IRISH SETTER

Susan Edwins has written a book that will be welcomed by all owners of the Irish Setter, both actual and potential. The latter will find it invaluable in helping them decide if the Irish Setter is the right dog for them, while the former—for whom there can be no other dog—will find it full of practical advice. The whole book, with its clear instructions on such matters as feeding, training, showing and breeding, will be found useful by owners of breeds other than the Irish Setter.

THE
IRISH SETTER

SUSAN M. EDWINS

FOYLES HANDBOOKS
LONDON

ISBN 0 7071 0701 6

© *W. & G. Foyle Ltd. 1980*

Published in Great Britain by
W. & G. Foyle Ltd.,
125 Charing Cross Road,
London WC2H 0EB

Photoset and printed in Great Britain by
Photobooks (Bristol) Ltd.,

CONTENTS

ILLUSTRATIONS

FOREWORD

Air Commodore J. A. Cecil-Wright, AFC, TD, AE

I was pleased to accept the author's invitation to write a foreword to her book. However, I find my task so much lighter because she herself has already done it so very well in her opening chapter 'Your First Irish Setter'. If her clear warnings could be digested by all those who are contemplating owning a dog for the first time, we would not, I am sure, be distressed so often by stories of abandoned and starving strays, many of which have to be destroyed. I congratulate her on this introduction, which shows her to be a true dog lover. The whole book, with its clear instructions for the novice, although addressed to potential buyers of Red Setters, is equally applicable to all breeds, and I strongly recommend it.

1

YOUR FIRST IRISH SETTER

THE IRISH SETTER is one of the most beautiful of all dogs and for those who own one there can be no other dog. As a breed it is fast gaining in popularity. This book is for those who are contemplating acquiring or have recently acquired one.

Advantages and disadvantages

Those people who have not yet become owners, but are considering doing so, should first consider the advantages and disadvantages of the Irish Setter.

Size This is one of the most important things to consider. An Irish Setter puppy is small and cuddly, but the dog can reach 27 inches to the shoulder.

Exercise As well as being somewhat large, these dogs need a great deal of exercise if they are to be healthy and happy. An under-exercised Setter will be constantly restless and boisterous, so if you are not prepared to devote some time every day to exercising it, do not contemplate buying one. The Irish Setter is not the dog for you if you live in a flat or a small house without a garden. Do not think of having one either if you are going to leave it on its own for long periods of time. Being highly intelligent, these dogs quickly become bored if left alone for too long, and the inevitable result of boredom is destructiveness!

Behaviour All puppies are naturally high-spirited and mischievous, so if you are likely to want to part with it at its first misdemeanour, then please think again about owning a dog of any kind. It may seem incredible to the majority of us, but any veterinary surgeon will tell you that, almost daily, people take young and healthy dogs along to be destroyed for extremely trivial reasons, such as licking the baby's hand, wetting the carpet, or inflated reports in the media regarding rabies and toxicara. To have a dog is the same as to have a child—it is yours, for better or for worse, and should remain with you for its entire life, except in the most rare and unforeseen circumstances.

Cost   Can you afford to keep an Irish Setter? An adult setter will eat 1½ to 2lb of meat daily, plus biscuit, so do make sure. Consider also the fact that veterinary fees can be expensive, and there are bound to be times when you will have to call upon the vet's services, although various insurance policies are available to cover accident and illness. You can also insure for third party risk in case your dog should cause an accident, for instance. Certain other expenses will also arise, such as a dog licence at six months of age, Kennel Club fees, or the occasional stay at boarding kennels. The Irish Setter needs grooming, and you will have to trim him every month or so for his own comfort, so you will have to devote a certain amount of time to this.

Management   You will need to be firm with the dog right from the start, before he decides that he is 'leader of the pack' and you are the underdog! Don't have an Irish Setter if you feel that you cannot assert yourself. You will probably be well advised to take him to obedience classes, so do take all this into account. There are other drawbacks—some dogs are car sick, which can be most inconvenient, and although Irish Setters are generally clean and fastidious, you will have to be patient while he is being house trained. Please consider also the cost of making sure that your garden is adequately fenced.

Dog or bitch?
Well, I do hope that the foregoing remarks have not deterred you, but it is as well to give them some consideration. Once you have made up your mind to have an Irish Setter, the next thing you have to decide is whether you want a dog or a bitch. There are things to be said for and against both, so let us consider them.

Dogs grow bigger than bitches, and are generally more of a handful. They are strong and need a very firm hand. Dogs will naturally have the wandering instinct, particularly if they can smell a bitch in season.

The main disadvantage with bitches is that they come into season approximately twice a year. The season lasts about four weeks and during this time the bitch will have to be confined to your house and garden in order to avoid a misalliance, the consequences of which can be costly and inconvenient. There are various products on the market which aim to neutralize the smell of an in-season bitch, but they do not completely eliminate the problem. In every other respect, the bitch is probably easier to deal with than the dog. Smaller, quieter, and on the whole more affectionate, bitches make ideal companions for people for whom the rather more independent nature of the dog would prove too much.

Of course, both dogs and bitches can be neutered, which is the ideal solution for those who do not propose to exhibit or breed their dogs. The operation is simpler for a dog than for a bitch, and should not be performed until the dog is six months old, or in the case of a bitch, until she has had her first season.

Showing
The next point to consider is whether you intend to show or work your Setter or whether it is to be purely a pet. A properly trained Irish Setter makes an excellent working gundog. Obviously, you will have to train the dog yourself for this purpose, or send it away to a specialist for training.

If you wish to buy an Irish Setter for show, then it will pay you to go to one of the top breeders for a puppy, or maybe a young adult which has been 'run on' in order to assess its potential. Showing is infectious, and once you taste success, however small, you will want to continue, so be warned!

Even if you are definitely not intending to show the dog, you will be well advised to go to a reputable breeder. Addresses of specialist breeders can be obtained from the Kennel Club, or you can speak to the breeders themselves by visiting one of the large championship dog shows, details of which are published weekly in *Our Dogs* and *Dog World*.

Buy a healthy and sound specimen which conforms as closely as possible to the breed standard. Many people who buy Irish Setters as pets later change their minds and decide to try their hand at showing. Obviously, if the dog you have bought is a sound and typical example of the breed, the better your chances of success in the show ring.

Choosing your puppy

Having decided whether your dog is going to be worked, shown or kept as a pet only, all that remains is to contact a breeder and go along to see some puppies, or maybe a couple of slightly older dogs. It may be advisable to go and see several litters and make some comparisons. Do take note of how the puppies are being kept, whether they look clean and free from fleas and lice, and whether there is any discharge from the eyes or nose. Do not be surprised if the breeder asks you not to handle the puppies, for every precaution has to be taken to safeguard them from outside infection. Take a look at the mother of the puppies and compare her in your mind to the breed standard.

Many people will tell you to choose the puppy which comes to you most readily, and at all costs to avoid the one which seems quiet and reserved, as this one, they say, may have a nervous disposition and could be unsuitable as a pet. If you are looking for a puppy as a pet, do not take too much notice of this theory. Every litter, after all, has its hierarchy, and inevitably one or more of the puppies will bully a couple of the others. These apparent 'underdogs' may blossom once they have been taken from the litter and allowed to develop their own personalities. There is no reason to suppose that they will be unduly shy or nervous once removed from bullying brothers and sisters. However, a very obviously quiet or nervous puppy could possibly be unsuitable for working or showing, so bear this in mind.

Do not assume that the smaller puppies are always the weaklings. Often the smaller puppies are very lively, highly intelligent, and as robust as any of the others as long as they are obviously healthy.

What you can expect to pay

At the time of writing I should say that the very least you can expect to pay for an Irish Setter puppy would be £50 to £60. Top breeders will undoubtedly ask considerably more. Many breeders will only sell puppies to intending exhibitors, and some may suggest having the dog on 'breeding terms'. This is an agreement made between breeder and purchaser whereby the latter has the dog at something less than the asking price subject to a set of conditions.

These conditions will vary a great deal. The purchaser may be asked, for instance, to promise to show the dog and breed from it under conditions laid down by the breeder. If a dog, it may be required to mate certain bitches specified by the breeder, who will probably want the first couple of stud fees once the dog's fertility has been proved. If you buy a bitch on breeding terms, you may be required to mate her to a specified dog and to supply several of the puppies or the sale price of them. Usually, the dog or bitch becomes yours once the conditions laid down have been complied with. If you do have a puppy on these terms, do make sure there is a written agreement made in order to avoid later misunderstandings.

If you are buying a puppy which is not yet old enough to leave the litter, you will be required to put down a deposit. This will vary from breeder to breeder, but one-third of the asking price would be a fair estimate. Once you have chosen your puppy and put down a deposit, all that remains is to make sure that you have all that is necessary ready for the new member of the family.

2

NOW HE'S YOURS

PUPPIES ARE READY to leave the nest at eight weeks of age, seldom before. Before collecting your puppy you will need to buy various things to have ready for him. A bed (preferably a large cardboard box to start with), some old blankets, feeding bowls, a water bowl, collar and lead, a brush and comb, and a stock of food and diet supplements. It is a good idea to ask the breeder for a copy of the diet sheet before you actually bring him home, so that you can stock up beforehand with the recommended foods.

Bringing your puppy home
When you go to collect your puppy, take some newspaper and old towels in the car with you in case he is car sick during the journey home. You should receive from the breeder:

1. Receipt for what you have paid.
2. Certificate of pedigree.
3. Diet sheet.
4. Kennel Club registration certificates and transfer of ownership form. The registration certificate may not always be immediately available, as sometimes they take some time to process, so don't forget to leave your address with the breeder so that these can be posted to you. Once you receive the registration you will probably wish to fill in the transfer form and send it off to the Kennel Club so that the dog can be properly transferred to your name. If you wish to show and/or breed from the dog its name must go on to the Kennel Club 'Active' Register. Some breeders don't register puppies themselves, and in this case it will be up to you to register the dog yourself. The Kennel Club can advise you in this instance.
5. Certificate of worming (most breeders will supply this on request).

If the puppy is under twelve weeks of age, it is unlikely to have been inoculated against distemper and leptospirosis (infectious canine jaundice). Most vets will not give these injections until the puppy is ten to twelve weeks old for the first dose and twelve to fourteen weeks old for the second. Booster injections will be needed annually. On no account must the puppy mix with other dogs or go anywhere other dogs have been until he has received both injections. This means that he must meet no other dogs, even in his own home, unless you already have another dog in the family, in which case the movements of that dog must be restricted to your own ground until the puppy is properly immune.

First night in his new home
The first night in his new home will obviously be strange for the puppy. He will miss the warmth and company of his brothers and sisters. Make sure that his bed is warm and draught-free (the kitchen is probably the best place for him to sleep). If you cut out one side of a large cardboard box and place some newspaper and old blankets in it, this should be quite adequate. If you buy him a wicker basket he will probably chew it to pieces, so it is best not to give him one of these until he has outgrown the chewing stage!

It is an excellent idea to place a warm hot-water bottle, wrapped in blankets, in the bed, and place nearby (but well out of reach) a ticking alarm-type clock. These will give the puppy some comfort —the warmth of the bottle will help to compensate for the lost heat of litter brothers and sisters, and the ticking of the clock will resemble the mother's heartbeat.

Do make sure that all electric flexes are well out of the puppy's reach. Line the floor with newspaper, as there will inevitably be at least a puddle to contend with in the morning. Leave some clean water down for him.

He will probably cry during the night, and if he does so for long, do go down and comfort him. But you must also be firm, and if he keeps on you will have to reproach him and tell him to be quiet, for puppies are like babies: if they get their own way too often they will know they are on to a good thing!

House training

With regard to house training, kindness is the key word right from
the start. You will be well rewarded. Put the puppy outside after
every meal and whenever he looks as though he is about to 'spend a
penny' indoors, and he will soon get the message, especially if he is
praised warmly when he does what you want him to. If you always
use the same encouragement, you may be able to teach him to
spend a penny on command, which can prove very useful. You
may have to scold him if he is persistently dirty indoors, but try to
avoid smacking him, except in dire circumstances. Remember that
a puppy will not understand what he has done wrong unless you
catch him in the act and scold him there and then.

Feeding

Follow as closely as possible the diet sheet given you by the
breeder, but do not worry too much if the puppy does not always
want to eat all that is given him. Appetites vary from dog to dog,
and whereas some dogs will invariably be greedy, others will be
finicky. Of course, veterinary advice should be sought if the dog
refuses to eat, or eats very little for more than a couple of days in
succession.

Health and general care

When you take the puppy along for his inoculations, ask the vet
for advice about worming. The puppy should have been properly
wormed by the breeder, but will still need worming at regular six-
monthly intervals—against roundworm in the case of puppies and
tapeworm in adult dogs.

Mention must be made here of *Toxicara Canis*, a condition
which has recently attracted much publicity. *Toxicara Canis* can be
caught by human beings as a result of contact with canine worms
and their eggs. In very rare cases it can cause partial blindness, but
it must be stressed that the chances of contracting the disease are
extremely minute and, if the usual standards of hygiene are
maintained, the risk is negligible. It is not possible to become
infected by dogs which are wormed regularly. Make sure that
children especially wash their hands after playing with the puppy,
etc.

Try not to become alarmed by the mass anti-dog hysteria that now seems to be common in some quarters. Like a lot of other things, the matter has been somewhat exaggerated by some who are not in possession of the true facts.

Your dog's nails will need cutting once in a while, and it is best to let the vet advise you about this, as it is a somewhat delicate procedure. Great care must be taken not to cut the quicks, as pain and bleeding will result if you do. For some dogs, a certain amount of roadwork will help to keep the nails short, but others will still need to have their nails cut despite daily exercise on concrete. Special nail clippers are available for dogs, but do get advice from someone knowledgeable before attempting the operation. Pay special attention to keeping the feet clean, especially between the toes, in order to prevent pedal eczema.

Get your puppy used to a collar as soon as possible. He will doubtless try to remove it by scratching, but if he wears it for a few minutes each day he will soon get used to it and accept it happily by the time he is old enough to go for walks. It is the law that dogs, when not on their own property, must wear a collar with name and address attached. However, while the dog is at home it is not a good idea to make him wear one all the time. Collars can be dangerous, as they can become hooked onto various things, and will cause the dog to struggle, which could result in strangulation. Collars can also cause an ugly mark around the neck, which does not look good if you are going to show the dog.

Exercise
As regards exercise, a short walk on the lead and a short run off the lead daily should be ample for a puppy under the age of six months. Indeed, over-exercising a youngster of this age can be harmful, as his bones are still soft and malleable, and damage can result. From the age of six to seven months onwards the dog will need more exercise, with plenty of free running, off the lead.

Of course, you must never let the dog off the lead anywhere near a road. He will need some free running every day, but make sure that this is somewhere well away from roads. If you are worried that the dog will run away and that you won't be able to catch him, exercise him on a long piece of rope (a 'wander lead') to start with.

When you do let him off the lead, call him and praise him enthusiastically if he responds to your call. Once he knows that he receives praise for coming back to you, he should be anxious to please. Don't just call him back when you want to put him on the lead, or he will connect the two and may not be so willing to come to you.

Do keep proper control over your dog in public places. Be extra careful about controlling him when near to farm land. He must never be allowed to trample down crops or worry cattle, sheep, or other livestock. Many farmers will not hesitate to shoot a dog which is worrying animals and they are legally entitled to do so.

Grooming and trimming

Basic requirements for grooming and trimming your dog are: brush and comb, thinning scissors, and sharp hairdressing scissors, usually obtainable from good pet shops or at dog shows. Five minutes' brushing every day should be quite sufficient, while the ears and featherings should be combed through once or twice a week to prevent matting. Please do not think that only show Setters need trimming—this is just not so. The ears (especially under the earflaps) and feet will need trimming once a month or so, for the dog's comfort.

It will do your dog no harm to receive the occasional bath, especially if he has rolled in something unpleasant, but he should not be bathed more than once or twice a year, as otherwise you will wash all the natural oils out of his coat. Used a medicated dog shampoo, and be sure to rinse properly and dry thoroughly. If you suspect fleas, you can dust the coat with one of the recognized powders, or bath him. If fleas persist, a flea collar may have to be resorted to.

Coming into season

If yours is a bitch, you can expect her to come into season at any time from five months of age onwards. Some may not have their first season until they are over a year old, but if your bitch reaches the age of eighteen month's and there has been no sign of her

Opposite: Trimming the ears–a monthly operation.

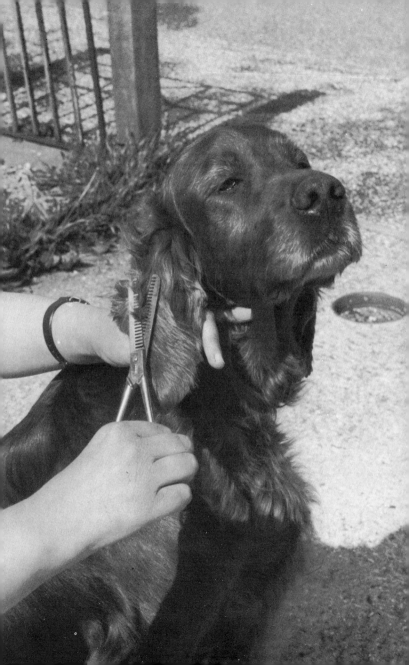

coming into season, veterinary advice should be sought as there may be some hormonal disturbance. Do not take her out during the time she is in season—this usually lasts for about four weeks.

The first sign that the bitch is commencing this fertile period is some slight swelling of the vulva, followed by a red discharge. The swelling and discharge will increase, and at about ten to fourteen days from the onset the discharge will become colourless. This is generally the most fertile time. After this time the vulva slowly returns to its normal size, which will be at about twenty-eight days.

It is best to confine the bitch for the whole of this time, as in some cases bitches are fertile right up to the end of the season, while others reach peak fertility at the end of this period and not around the usual twelfth day.

General training
You will need to be firm with your puppy right from the word go. A bad habit which he is likely to develop is jumping up, so this must be discouraged from the beginning. If he does so, push him down immediately and praise him once he has got down. If you wish to ban him from jumping on furniture, you must stop him from doing so right from the start.

He will feel the need to chew, especially when, at about five months of age, he loses his puppy teeth, so provide him with some dog chews. Never give him anything which could be dangerous if swallowed. If he is given rubber toys, impress on him that although these are his to chew, your best shoes do not fall into the same category! Keep an eye on him if he has a bone or a dog chew, as bits of these very occasionally become stuck in the throat and could cause him to choke.

Pulling on the lead can cause problems and can also be difficult to stop once the habit has been established. When the puppy has received all his vaccinations, make enquiries about obedience classes. These can generally commence at approximately four to six months of age. Your local vet should be able to tell you who to contact regarding obedience classes. At these classes both you and the dog will receive training, and this should help with pulling and other problems.

You can start 'Ring craft' classes (training classes for would-be show dogs) also at four to six months old. Your local canine society should be able to inform you about these classes. If you need the address of your nearest canine society, the Kennel Club should be able to advise you.

3

FEEDING

THE BREEDER should have provided you with a diet sheet for your puppy, but in case you are without one here is a sample diet sheet for puppies of two to six months old.

Four meals a day

   Meal 1   Cereal (Farex, porridge, Weetabix or similar) with milk and a little glucose.

   Meal 2   Meat and biscuit. The meat should be varied. Recommended meats are minced beef, tripe or pet mince, raw or cooked, ox cheek, ox heart or similar. Tinned meat may be given, but it is advisable to feed fresh meat a couple of times a week. Liver should be fed sparingly for it can cause diarrhoea.

   The amount of meat should increase as the puppy grows. At eight weeks the puppy will eat approximately $\frac{3}{4}$ to 1lb of meat daily, increasing gradually, so that at six months of age a dog will eat $1\frac{1}{2}$ to $2\frac{1}{2}$lb of meat daily and a bitch slightly less. A fully-grown Irish Setter dog should receive about the same amount of meat ($1\frac{1}{2}$ to $2\frac{1}{2}$lb.) and a bitch $1\frac{1}{2}$ to 2lb, although this will vary according to the size and appetite of the individual. A correctly fed Irish Setter should have a nicely rounded appearance, racy but not ribby, and never fat.

   With the meat there should be biscuit (puppy meal), which should be pre-soaked and mixed with the meat in the ratio approximately two parts meat to one part biscuit. Puppy meal can be bought in 56lb bags. Many breeders and owners of Irish Setters feed puppy meal to their adult dogs in preference to the larger biscuit because of the occasional instance of bloat (dilation and twisting of the stomach) which can occur as a result of food swelling up in the stomach after meals, but opinions vary about this.

Opposite: Relaxation.

Meal 3   Same as Meal 2, the total daily allowance to be divided between the two meat meals.

Meal 4   Cereal, or a bowl of warm milk.

Extra vitamin and mineral supplements

These should be given up to the age of six months and sometimes afterwards. A calcium supplement, such as Stress, Canovel or SA 37, is essential and obtainable from any pet shop. Dosage as marked on the tin or packet. In addition, Vetzyme, Vitapet or cod liver oil can be given.

Eggs   An occasional raw egg, mixed with the cereal, is beneficial, but should not be given more than once or twice a week.

Fish   Can occasionally be substituted for meat, but always cook first and be sure to check that you have removed all the bones.

Bones   If bones are given, they must be marrow bones, as other types tend to splinter, with serious consequences.

Fresh water   This should be available at all times. Dog bowls should be washed daily.

From the age of about four months the puppy may show some reluctance to eat some of his meals, especially the cereal, so do not force the issue. The number of meals can be cut down gradually. Many adult dogs receive just one meat and biscuit meal daily, but two, smaller, meals may be better for the dog and can help to prevent bloat.

The occasional titbit does no harm, and chocolate drops contain vitamins as well as being a nice treat. As long as one is sensible, a few titbits and table scraps are permissible, provided that what is given is wholesome, for example, raw or cooked vegetables. It is not a good idea, though, to allow the dog to remain in the room when you are eating a meal.

4

HEALTH

A DEGREE OF common sense is the most important factor when dealing with the general care and health of your Irish Setter. Do not be afraid to consult your veterinary surgeon if you are in any way worried. The most important ingredients for a healthy, happy dog are adequate food of the right type, with care not to overfeed, a constant supply of clean drinking water, regular grooming, and plenty of exercise. The emotional needs of the dog should not be ignored either. A loving and affectionate relationship with human companions is essential.

Hereditary conditions

Although the Irish Setter is no more prone to illness than any other breed of dog, certain hereditary conditions have been known in the breed. The most notorious of these must be Progressive Retinal Atrophy, otherwise known as 'night blindness' or PRA, which nearly destroyed the breed earlier in this century. Thanks to the integrity of Irish Setter breeders of that time, the condition is now quite rare in the breed.

Hip Dysplasia is something which occasionally appears, although it is not common in the breed. The condition arises when the head of the femur fails to fit properly into the pelvis, and this can cause great pain and suffering. The degree of affliction varies a great deal. The milder cases can be controlled by a careful diet, avoidance of excessive exercise, and veterinary care.

Entropion is an inward turning of the eyelids. There again, this can occur in varying degrees of severity. The worst cases cause the lower eyelashes to irritate the eyeball, thus causing constant discomfort and watering of the eyes. The condition is operable.

All these conditions are usually in some way hereditary, although the exact mode of inheritance is not always known. However, it is never advisable to breed from any animal which has one of these afflictions as they are liable to be passed on, thus doing much harm to the breed.

Common ailments

Listed below are some of the common, as well as some of the not-so-common, ailments which can occur, some of which are more acute than others.

Abscesses These usually develop as a result of a deep puncture wound, a dog bite for example, whereby the wound becomes contaminated and a painful swelling develops. They can occur anywhere on the body. The safest thing is to take the dog to the vet, who may drain the abscess and administer antibiotics.

Anaemia Iron deficiency is usually the cause of anaemia, which manifests itself by loss of pigment, especially around the nose, and a general run down condition. Veterinary advice should be sought.

Anal glands Occasionally the glands on each side of the anus become blocked and if the condition is not treated an abscess can result. If the glands do block, the dog may be seen pulling itself along on its bottom, as though it had worms. Another sign is chewing around the tail area. A vet can easily express the glands, with gentle pressure. In order to avoid the trouble involved, make sure the dog has plenty of roughage in its diet and ample exercise.

Bad breath This is usually a sign of an upset stomach, bad teeth or wrong feeding. If Amplex tablets or charcoal granules in the feed do not help, consult the vet.

Balanitis An infection of the male sex organ, with discharge of pus and irritation. Ointment is available from the vet.

Bloat This is an acute condition in which the stomach dilates and twists and can quickly be fatal if veterinary treatment is not sought immediately. It often occurs after a meal, especially if the meal is dry and water is taken during or after eating. The food in the stomach swells, the stomach rotates so that both ends are blocked, gas builds up inside the stomach, and the organ may rupture. It is a mistake, however, to assume that this can only happen after meals, or that feeding pre-soaked food will always prevent its occurrence, as the condition has often been known to occur some hours before or after a meal, and when no water has been given. If the dog has bloat it will often drool and try to vomit and respirations may be laboured. The abdomen will be noticeably swollen and taut. Waste no time—phone the vet and get the dog to him as soon as possible, as every second will count. If you are quick, a tragedy may be averted.

Constipation Usually a result of lack of roughage in the diet. Do not assume that, because the dog's motions appear hard, he is constipated. This is a normal canine motion. If, however, the dog is seen to be straining and you are quite sure that no motion has been passed, then there could be some form of blockage such as a piece of bone, see your vet.

Diarrhoea Constantly runny motions are not a normal phenomenon and are usually the result of wrong feeding or a bowel infection. First of all, stop feeding all meat and substitute rice pudding. If this does not remedy the situation within a day or so, seek advice. If the motions are bloodstained, seek immediate help as this can be serious.

Distemper This condition is highly contagious—look out for cold-like symptoms, together with vomiting and loss of appetite, diarrhoea, runny eyes and excessive salivation. The condition is most common in young puppies which have not yet been vaccinated and is highly unlikely once the dog has been properly inoculated and received all its boosters. If treatment is delayed, permanent brain and/or nerve damage may result.

Ear troubles These are sometimes referred to as 'canker'. Ear infections have a number of causes, such as mites and wax. They will be made obvious by the presence of a dark-brown discharge and offensive smell, and the dog will constantly scratch its ears. If the condition is neglected, haematoma (a large blood blister in the ear flap) may result, necessitating surgical intervention. Incidentally, never attempt to probe your dog's ears with any form of instrument.

Eczema There are various types of eczema, with different causes. In some cases parasites may be responsible, while other types may be due to hormonal disturbance. The dog is constantly scratching and biting its skin and hair will doubtless be lost in some areas. The condition may take a long time to put right, so do not delay in seeking veterinary advice. Pedal eczema is often due to harvest mites.

Epilepsy   If the dog starts to have fits they could be due to epilepsy, which can develop at any age. The condition can be controlled, but not cured, and diagnosis can only be made by a vet. Never breed from a known epileptic as the condition is often hereditary.

Eye troubles   Any eye discharge should be treated by the vet. There can be various causes, such as foreign bodies, scratches or infection. Constantly running eyes are not normal and could be a sign of entropion, so do seek expert advice.

False pregnancy   Any unspayed bitch can develop a false pregnancy at around the time she would normally have whelped had she been pregnant. The usual signs are enlargement of the mammary glands, often accompanied by milk, and behaviour as though she were in whelp. The bitch may even go through a false labour and adopt some object as a 'puppy'. Unfortunately, if the bitch is inclined to false pregnancies, it is likely that she will develop one after every season in varying degrees of severity. Even if she is bred from, she is still liable to develop the condition on the occasions when she is not in whelp. Treatment can be given by way of hormone tablets and general cutting down of fluid intake. Some vets advocate spaying if the bitch suffers from repeated and severe false pregnancies.

Fits   These can be due to epilepsy, but there are other causes such as poisoning or food allergy. They can also occur as an aftermath of distemper, so of course you must consult your vet.

Jaundice   A symptom rather than a disease in itself, the first signs of jaundice are yellow discolouration of eyes, lips and skin. Jaundice can be a sign of liver malfunction, worms, or leptospirosis. Protection from the last of these is generally given as part of the routine inoculation for distemper.

Mange   This condition is nowadays easier to treat. The cause is a tiny mite and the loss of patches of hair is generally the first sign of its presence, usually on the edges of the ears, in the armpits and back of hind legs. It is associated with intense irritation.

Opposite: A healthy Setter in a natural pose.

Misalliance Vigilance is the key word when your bitch is in season. If you take her out, do not let her off the lead, and do not let her run unsupervised in the garden, as a dog will often travel a long way after an in-season bitch and a gate or fence will act as no deterrent to a determined suitor. If you have reason to suspect that your bitch has been mated and you do not wish her to have pups, she can be given an injection, which must be given within about thirty-six hours, to prevent her from having puppies, so do not delay in contacting your vet.

Parasites

Fleas These are something which attack most dogs from time to time. If you find evidence of fleas—flea deposits are black specks which when moistened become reddish-coloured—in your dog's coat, try dusting with one of the proprietary brands of dusting powder. If this is of no avail, a bath, using medicated shampoo, may do the trick. As a final resort, a flea collar may have to be purchased; this should not be worn by a nursing bitch, however, as close contact with this could be harmful to young puppies. Do not forget that, when using dusting powder, the dog's sleeping quarters must also be treated.

Lice These may initially be noticeable by their eggs, which are small, yellowish and oblong, and adhere to the dog's hair. Treatment is similar to that for fleas, but if in doubt consult the vet.

Ticks If your dog has been running in long grass or in any rural area, it is quite likely that at some time or other a tick may attach itself to some part of the dog's anatomy. Ticks are easily recognized by their fleshy appearance. They can be pink or grey in colour. They embed their heads under the dog's skin and suck the blood. Removal of these pests can be tricky, as if the head of the tick is left under the skin an abscess may result. A swab of cotton wool, soaked in surgical spirit, methylated spirit or alcohol will usually do the trick, causing the tick to release its grasp.

Harvest mites These usually cause intense irritation and are usually to be found as orange specks on the skin between the toes. They generally respond if treated with flea powder.

Worms The most common kinds of worms are roundworms

and tapeworms. Roundworms are usually associated with puppies, seldom with older dogs. They are long and thin, resembling fine spaghetti. Puppies are usually born with round-worms, which are passed from the mother. Worming of puppies before they leave the litter, and then once or twice before they reach maturity, should eliminate the problem. Tapeworms gener-ally only affect older dogs and are flat and segmented. There again, routine six-monthly wormings are the solution. Worms in general are difficult to diagnose, unless from a faeces sample, as symptoms are similar to those of other conditions. However, signs can be general malaise, dull coat, increased appetite and running the bottom along the ground; but do consult your vet, as all these things could be symptomatic of something else.

Pyometra A condition in bitches in which pus builds up in the womb over a period of time. It is most common in elderly maiden bitches or those who have had only one litter and is sometimes linked with frequent false pregnancies. The bitch drinks water excessively and there is sometimes a discharge of pus from the womb; also fever and loss of appetite. Prompt veterinary attention is needed, and in most cases a hysterectomy has to be performed.

Travel sickness A few Irish Setters are prone to this. To avoid it, do not feed the dog for some hours prior to a journey. Travel sickness pills can also help. The old remedy of dragging a small chain from the back bumper of the car has been known to work. It is a good idea to take the dog on frequent short car rides which culminate in a pleasurable experience, such as a run in the country, thus associating car rides with something enjoyable.

Vaginal discharge Other than normal in-season discharge, vaginal discharge can have various causes—pyometra, for example. Occasionally it occurs in young puppies and in this instance may be due to infection or the influence of hormones in the mother's milk.

First aid
Do remember that an animal in pain is liable to bite even its owner, so it may be necessary to apply a temporary muzzle. A tie or headscarf will do in an emergency. Make a slip knot in the centre

and put the noose over the dog's muzzle. Pull the noose tight enough to keep the jaws shut. The long ends should then be looped around the back of the head and tied behind the ears.

Bites Bathe with warm water. If the wound is a fairly large one, seek veterinary advice. Otherwise, keep the affected area clean.

Bleeding Excessive external bleeding from any kind of wound requires emergency treatment. If veterinary help is not immediately at hand, place some kind of pad over the site of bleeding and apply direct pressure at the bleeding point. If the bleeding is from the ear, this can look more serious than it actually is. The best way to deal with this is to place a pad on top of the dog's head, fold the affected ear over the top and bandage in place, using the other ear as an anchor for the bandage.

Burns and scalds Shock, resulting from a burn or scald, can be as harmful—if not more so—than the burn itself, so do not delay seeking veterinary treatment unless the burn is a small one. As an emergency measure, bathe immediately with cold water or tea. Do *not* apply butter, or any form of grease, as this renders it more difficult to treat.

Cuts and other wounds As with animal bites, the area should be cleaned and appropriate action taken if there is much bleeding. Veterinary treatment may be necessary, as stitches may be required. Bandaging can be difficult, as the dog may try to remove it, and bandaged feet can be especially so as the dressings will quickly become dirty, so a plastic bag may have to be tied over the bandage. Do not use rubber bands to secure this.

Choking If a bone or something similar becomes lodged across the roof of the mouth between the teeth, you can remove it by hand if you are able to. But a lower obstruction which can cause the dog to choke will require emergency treatment. The best way to deal with this initially is to support the dog's hindquarters, so that the head hangs down, and apply a sharp blow to the chest area. If this fails to dislodge the object, a general anaesthetic will be needed.

Drowning If a young puppy, support the hindquarters with the head hanging downwards, clear the mouth and throat of any obstruction such as mud, pull the tongue forwards, and then fairly rapidly compress the chest to restore breathing. If there is no detectable heartbeat this may be restored by rapidly compressing

Friends both sitting

. . . and standing!

Head study

Setter with young friend

the chest wall at a point just behind the elbow. An adult dog should be placed on a slope, or with the hindquarters raised on a support, with the tongue pulled well forward before artificial respiration is applied.

Electric shock   Usually caused by the dog's chewing through an electric flex. Disconnect current before touching the dog, or you will also get a shock. If the dog appears to have stopped breathing, apply external cardiac massage, as described under drowning.

Heatstroke and sunstroke   Excessive panting in hot weather, followed by a collapsed state, especially if the dog has been outside without much shade, are sure signs of sunstroke or heatstroke, and the simple remedy is to hose the dog down or completely immerse it, apart from its head, in cold water. In the case of tiny puppies, make sure that their accommodation does not become overheated for they cannot regulate their body temperature as well as older dogs. If they are constantly crying during hot weather for no apparent reason, this could well be the cause. Immerse them gently for a couple of seconds in cold water (keeping the heads above water), then gently towel them dry and put them in a cool place. Please be alert to the risk of leaving a dog shut in a car during sunny weather.

Insect bites and stings   If the bite is an external one, bathe the area with a solution of vinegar in the case of a wasp sting or bicarbonate of soda if a bee sting. In the latter case remove the sting. You must rush the dog to the vet if the bite is inside the mouth, as the resulting swelling could impair breathing and prove fatal.

Poisoning   If you know or suspect that your dog has swallowed something poisonous, you must act quickly. Push washing soda down the dog's throat; if none is available, try to get him to swallow as much salt water as possible, in order to get him to vomit, and call the vet immediately.

Shock   This often follows some other trauma and needs urgent treatment. Keep the animal warm and quiet. Give nothing by mouth in case a general anaesthetic is necessary.

Snake bites   Adder bites are often less serious than generally thought, but always seek veterinary advice if only to put your mind at rest. The usual consequence of an adder bite is some degree of swelling around the site. As in the case of bee or wasp stings, if the mouth or throat is involved the situation can rapidly become serious, so seek immediate veterinary assistance. For any other kinds of snake bite do not delay: get the dog to a vet.

5

BASIC LESSONS IN OBEDIENCE

IN ORDER to have a happy relationship with your Irish Setter some degree of training in obedience is essential. It is well said that a trained dog is a happy dog. When the puppy is still quite young you can start basic training by teaching him to sit and stay and to come to you when called. Be full of praise when he does what he is told, but do not shout at him or scold him if he does not get the message at first for you may frighten him. A great deal of patience is necessary on your part and care must be taken not to overtax a young puppy—five minutes of obedience training daily is quite enough to start with.

Make him sit by gently pulling his head up with the lead and pressing down on his quarters with the other hand until he is sitting down, at the same time telling him to sit and praising him when he does so. Nothing pleases a dog more than praise when he knows he has done well. The same thing applies to when you call him to you—if he knows that by coming to you he will be rewarded with praise you should have no trouble in getting him to do what is required of him. Never shout at him if he does not come back when called—scolding will only make him more reluctant to come back.

As mentioned in an earlier chapter, try to avoid only calling him to you when you want to put him back on the lead or he will naturally come to associate the two. Call him to you frequently, then let him run off again, until it is time to go back on the lead. When you wish him to stay in one place, move away from him gradually, telling him all the time to stay. Do not make him stay for too long at first, and be ready to reward him when he does well.

Obedience classes
When the puppy has mastered these simple lessons, which nevertheless may take quite some time to perfect, he will be ready to progress to more disciplined work. When he reaches this stage

you must be more firm with him and never give a command unless you intend it to be obeyed and are in a position to make sure it is. If a dog learns that it can disobey and get away with it, you have taken a backward step.

At this stage you would be well advised to acquire a specialist book on obedience, but probably the best way to teach your dog is to take him to obedience classes, where all the aforementioned points will be taught and put into practice by experts. You can start a puppy off at these classes when he is four to six months old. Your local dog training club will run these sessions, probably once a week. Your local vet will usually tell you who to contact regarding these classes.

You will need to buy a check chain or other type of slip lead. Ask someone knowledgeable as to the right and wrong ways of putting on a slip lead—no doubt whoever is in charge of the obedience classes will make a point of advising you in this matter. The check chain or lead must be put on so that it slackens when pressure is released, otherwise it will remain taut.

Obedience competitions

At obedience classes both dogs and their handlers are trained in basic obedience and slowly graduate into the more advanced classes. Basic training includes heel on the lead, sit, down, stay and recall, and when these have been mastered, the dog will learn to heel off the lead, retrieve objects and learn scent discrimination. If you wish to, you will be able to enter for obedience competitions, where you can initially enter your dog in the simple tests, and when these have been passed he can progress to the more advanced tests. The ultimate goal is the title of obedience champion. Apart from the sense of satisfaction that can be gained from winning awards for obedience, there is no doubt that the close rapport necessary between dog and owner can only serve to enhance the already happy relationship between them.

The Irish Setter is not a breed seen frequently competing in this field, although a number have done very well. Maybe his spirit of independence makes him more difficult to train initially, but if you

Opposite: Making him sit.

persevere with him you will be delighted at the way he responds and the pleasure he takes in working with you.

Gundog training

If you have bought your Irish Setter to work him to the gun, it will of course be necessary to start training him for this work as early as possible. If you have sufficient knowledge and experience you will be able to train the dog yourself, but if not you can send your dog away to be trained. Here he will learn the various skills required for his particular role. The Kennel Club or one of the breed clubs can no doubt supply you with the addresses of specialist trainers and gundog training clubs. You can also obtain various comprehensive books on the subject.

As well as working your dog privately, you can, when sufficiently competent, participate in Field Trials, which are a great test of your dog's natural skills.

The Setter's traditional role is to quarter the ground in advance of the guns, seeking out game and indicating its presence by 'setting', that is, freezing in one position and thereby 'hypnotising' the game until such time as the birds are driven into the air. This used to be the extent of the Setter's role, and Retrievers were then used to fetch the dead birds. However, these days the Irish Setter is often used as an all-round gundog and indeed he possesses excellent retrieving qualities, including a beautiful soft mouth. Some sportsmen in the past have not favoured the Irish Setter because of the rather independent nature of the breed, but once properly trained the Irish Setter makes an excellent hard-working and enthusiastic gundog.

6

SHOWING

You MAY have bought your Irish Setter with a view to showing him, or you may decide to do so later on. Whichever way you start, you will find showing interesting and worthwhile, especially when you have won your first card. It is pleasant meeting other people with the same love of the breed and many friendships begin this way.

You cannot show a puppy under the age of six months. Before you can do so, you will have to check that your Setter is registered with the Kennel Club and has been transferred to your name. It will also have to be on the Kennel Club 'Active' Register.

There is no point in showing a dog or bitch with obvious bad faults, such as black markings or an undershot/overshot mouth, the latter being failure of the incisors to meet in either an even or a 'scissor' bite. A serious fault in the case of a dog is bilateral cryptorchidism, in which neither testicle has descended into the scrotum. When only one testicle is present the condition is known as unilateral cryptorchidism; the dog can be shown, but will obviously be penalized. Sometimes one or both testicles can be as late as eighteen months in descending, but generally both should be present by nine to twelve months of age. You cannot show a castrated dog or a spayed bitch unless it has already produced one or more offspring which are registered with the Kennel Club.

Preparing for showing
It is a good idea to take your puppy to 'ring craft' classes from about the age of four months (your local canine society will supply you with information about these). Here your puppy will get used to being handled by strangers and mixing with other dogs, and you will be trained to show him to best advantage, which is just as important. You can practise at home, too, by making him 'stand' every day in correct show stance. When you take him out for a

walk, practise trotting him up and down on a loose lead, and this will get him used to the idea of moving in the show ring.

Initially, it may be a good idea to leave your dog at home and visit a show where classes are scheduled for Irish Setters. You can see how the dogs are handled and observe general show procedure, so that when you enter for your first show you will be a little more confident.

To find out where and when shows are being held, order a weekly copy of *Dog World* or *Our Dogs* from your newsagent. You will find all the information you require in these papers, together with show reports, interesting articles and photographs. When you decide that you and your dog are ready, send for a schedule; a small, local show will be a good idea to start with.

A show where there are classes scheduled for Irish Setters will be preferable, but if yours is a young puppy you may find that, if it is a small event, there are no classes for Irish Setter puppies. In this instance, you may have to enter him in 'Any Variety Gundog Puppy' or 'Any Variety Minor Puppy', or something similar. You will find the different classifications and their explanation listed in the schedule. Do make sure that you note the closing date for entries, or you may find that you have left it too late.

Types of shows

There are various types of shows. You can go to a small *exemption* show, where you can enter on the field on the day. Classes here generally include one for puppies of all breeds, Any Variety Sporting, Any Variety Non-Sporting, a Veteran Class and Novelty Classes. The latter include such light-hearted events as the dog with the most appealing expression or most waggly tail, but which are nevertheless good experience for both you and your dog.

Don't be too despondent, nevertheless, if you don't always get placed at exemption shows. They can attract a large number of dogs, especially on a sunny day, and as there are no breed classes your dog will be up against many different breeds. The judge cannot always be an expert on every breed of dog so you will

Opposite: Final judging in the arena at Crufts.

sometimes be disappointed, but the experience you gain will always be valuable.

For all other shows, entries must be made in advance. *Sanction* shows are small events where breeders generally take their puppies and young stock to give them their first experience of showing. *Limited* shows are slightly larger and are, as the name suggests, limited to members of the organising canine society. *Open* shows are much bigger and tend to attract bigger entries. *Championship* shows, of which Crufts is one, attract the largest number and highest quality of exhibits. Classes for Irish Setters are always divided into dogs and bitches—for example, puppy dog, puppy bitch, junior dog, and junior bitch—and the competition is invariably stiff. When the breed classes have been judged, the first prize winners of each class compete together for Best of Breed. For any dog to become a Show Champion it must win three Challenge Certificates (awarded to best dog of each sex) at championship shows under three different judges. To become a full Champion, an Irish Setter must qualify in the field as well as on the bench.

In the case of Crufts, it should be mentioned that one cannot enter this show as one would any other. It is necessary to qualify one's dog at a championship show during the preceding year. This is normally done by winning a first prize in certain classes, but requirements for Crufts qualification can vary from year to year, so if in doubt you should check with the Kennel Club.

Always read the show regulations carefully before sending off your entry. At many shows, and always at championship shows, you are expected to stay until a certain time specified in the schedule, although at smaller shows this is often not enforced. 'Early removals', allowing those living about 50 or more miles from the venue to leave an hour or so earlier, can be obtained if applied for at the time of sending in entries. You will need to obtain a show lead and a benching chain, the latter for use at shows where the exhibits are benched. These can usually be bought at the larger shows. Do buy a properly made swivel-type benching chain, as this is the only safe kind.

Grooming and trimming

Your dog's coat and featherings will need to be prepared for the show. Ears and feet will need thinning and trimming in order to make him look as attractive as possible. In the United Kingdom it is common to trim the ears, but in other countries—the United States for example—long hair on ears is preferred.

The best method of thinning hair is to pluck between finger and thumb, but this is a somewhat time-consuming business and most people have to do some trimming with scissors. This should be done at least a week before the show so that scissor marks will not be too apparent. A few finishing touches may nevertheless be necessary on the day prior to the show.

If you are going to bath the dog before the show, do so some days beforehand, or the coat may look 'fluffy' on the day of the show. Whatever you do, don't bath your Setter before every show you attend. As previously mentioned, too frequent bathing will destroy the natural oils in the dog's coat. So only bath when the occasion really demands and never more than two or three times a year.

Show Champion Hartsbourne Periwinkle (owner Miss S. Lennox).

If the person who bred your dog is an exhibitor, he or she will probably be willing to give some help and advice on trimming. Everyone has their own method of trimming an Irish Setter, but here is a general guide:

1.   Remove surplus hair from under the earflaps so that ears lie flat and close to the head.
2.   Thin hair from the outer ear leather. If thinning scissors are used, work upwards.
3.   Neaten round the edge of earflaps. Extreme caution is necessary here, as with all trimming. An accidental nip with the scissors could prove extremely traumatic.
4.   Trim a little hair from between the toes of all four feet.
5.   Remove some excess hair from bottom of feet, between pads. Take care not to remove too much, or there will be insufficient protection in between the pads.
6.   Neaten round edges of feet.
7.   Trim hair from below hocks (cut downwards).
8.   Optionally, thin hair between throat and breastbone.

Show Champion Stephenshill Gamebird (owner Mr N. W. Morrish).

In the United States this is done rather more thoroughly in order to produce a truly clean-throated appearance, but this practice is not favoured in the United Kingdom.

If you encounter any mats in your dog's coat, usually under earflaps or between legs, they should normally be cut out. Do not attempt to pull them out—imagine how painful this would be!

The earliest start with trimming pays dividends, so get your dog used to the idea while still quite young. Patience should pay off and regular sessions with brush and comb should get him well used to the procedure.

At the show

Now to the day of the show. Note from the schedule what time the show starts, and try to get there as early as possible. Dogs are not usually accepted after a certain hour. Just because your class looks to be one of the later ones, do not assume that it will not be judged until quite late. This may be the case, but it depends upon the number of rings available and weather conditions. Your class could turn out to be one of the first. At championship shows the judging of the numerically large breeds, such as Irish Setters, invariably starts early.

Make sure that you take everything you need—your Exhibitor's Pass and car park ticket, if these are being issued, and a 'show bag' containing all the necessary equipment (show lead, benching chain, grooming kit, blanket for your dog to lie on, water bowl and flask of water). You may also wish to take a thermos of coffee for yourself, and something to eat. If you haven't got a special clip to secure your ring number card, these can usually be bought at larger shows. At any rate, take a safety pin in case you cannot get a clip.

When you arrive at the show ground you will need to buy a catalogue. You can find out from this what your bench or ring number is, if you don't already know, and you will also be able to see at a glance how many entries there are in your class. If it is a benched show, put your dog on his bench as soon as possible to get him used to the idea. Make sure that you attach him securely with a proper benching chain (note how other people fix these). Always

Louian Quiller (owner Mrs J. Newberry).

Show Champion Wendover Gentleman (owner Mr and Mrs L. C. James).

make sure that your dog is wearing an ordinary collar—a benching chain should never be attached to a choke chain. Make sure that the benching chain is made short enough to prevent the dog from getting down or half down from the bench. Don't go away and leave your dog alone on his bench for too long, especially if this is the first time that he has been benched. Take him off the bench for a walk around every so often.

About half an hour before you are due to go in the ring, start to get your dog ready. Give him a final brush, and comb through the featherings on tail, tummy, chest and legs. Take him for a few practice runs up and down. He may need to relieve himself before going in the ring, so take him to one of the 'exercise areas' set aside for this purpose.

When your class is called, take your dog into the ring and collect your ring card from the steward. When all the dogs are in the ring and the judge is ready to commence, the handlers prepare their dogs for initial inspection. The aim is to get the dog to stand and show to best advantage while the judge is looking at him and to relax the rest of the time.

When the judge has looked round the ring at all the dogs, he may ask everyone to move their dogs around at a trot to get an initial idea of how each one moves. Then comes a closer inspection of each exhibit. Each dog in turn is taken up to the judge, who will generally start by studying the dog's profile, and will then give a more thorough examination. This will include a look at the teeth to check correct dentition, and an examination of bone, shoulders, ribs, quarters and general substance.

You will then be asked to move the dog, usually in a triangle and then straight up and down. A Setter will move to best advantage on a loose lead, thus giving him the freedom to really stretch out and show his marvellous driving action and slashing tail. Unfortunately not all dogs move as well as they should, but sometimes this can be made worse by being shown on too tight a lead. However, it is true that some dogs tend to pull away if allowed too much lead. Plenty of practice beforehand, especially at ring craft classes, should correct this.

When the judge is satisfied that he has thoroughly inspected your dog, return to the end of the line while he goes on to look at all

the other dogs. While the others are being examined you can allow your dog to relax. In shows where there are numerically large classes you may have to spend a long time in the ring so, to avoid restlessness and boredom, only make him 'stand to attention' when really necessary.

When the judge has seen all the dogs, he will then go around the ring looking at all the exhibits briefly before picking out the winners. This is the time when your dog must be made to look his best, so get him standing as well as you can. The judge will quietly indicate which dogs he wishes to be placed. Do not relax your dog until the steward says that the judge has 'finished with the rest'. There are usually five prize cards in each class, with a small cash prize for the first three.

If you have not been lucky enough to get placed, try not to be too disheartened. There will always be other shows and other judges. You may go to half a dozen shows without any success, but if you are prepared to keep trying then eventually the day will come when, maybe to your surprise, the judge beckons you into the centre of the ring. Your delight then will be immeasureable, and all your hard work will have proved worthwhile. Your dog, too, will sense that this is something special. From now on there will be no turning back.

Opposite: An informal showing!

7

THE BREED STANDARD

United Kingdom
The following is reproduced by kind permission of the British Kennel Club.

General Appearance   Must be racy, full of quality, and kindly in expression.

Head and skull   The head should be long and lean, not narrow or snipey, and not coarse at the ears. The skull oval (from ear to ear), having plenty of brain room, and with well-defined occipital protruberance. Brows raised, showing stop. The muzzle moderately deep, and fairly square at end. From the stop to the point of the nose should be long, the nostrils wide, and the jaws of nearly equal length, flews not to be pendulous. The colour of the nose: dark mahogany, or dark walnut, or black.

Eyes   Should be dark hazel or dark brown and ought not to be too large.

Ears   The ears should be of moderate size, fine in texture, set on low, well back, and hanging in a neat fold close to the head.

Mouth   Not over- or undershot.

Neck   Should be moderately long, very muscular, but not too thick, slightly arched, free from all tendency to throatiness.

Forequarters   The shoulders to be fine at the point, deep and sloping well back. The chest as deep as possible, rather narrow in front. The forelegs should be straight and sinewy, having plenty of bone, with elbows free, well let down, not inclined either in or out.

Body   Should be proportionate, the ribs well sprung, leaving plenty of lung room. Loins muscular, slightly arched.

Hindquarters   Should be wide and powerful. The hind legs from hip to hock should be long and muscular; from hock to heel short and strong. The stifle and hock joints well bent, and not inclined either in or out.

Opposite: Head study of a young bitch.

Feet   Should be small, very firm, toes strong, close together and arched.

Tail   Should be of moderate length, proportionate to the size of the body, set on rather low, strong at root, and tapering to a fine point; to be carried as nearly as possible on a level with or below the back.

Coat and feathering   On the head, front of the legs, and tips of the ears, should be short and fine, but on all other parts of the body and legs it ought to be of moderate length, flat, and as free as possible from curl or wave. The feather on the upper portion of the ears should be long and silky; on the back of fore and hind legs should be long and fine; a fair amount of hair on the belly, forming a nice fringe, which may extend on chest and throat. Feet to be well feathered between the toes. Tail to have a nice fringe of moderately long hair, decreasing in length as it approaches the point. All feathering to be as straight and as flat as possible.

Colour   The colour should be rich chestnut, with no trace whatever of black; white on chest, throat or toes, or a small star on the forehead, or a narrow streak or blaze on the nose or face not to disqualify.

Diagram showing points of the breed.

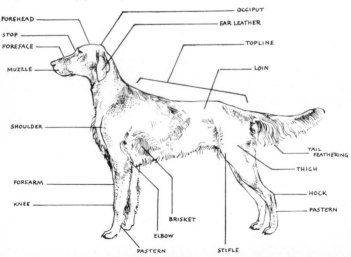

United States
The following is reproduced by kind permission of the American Kennel Club.

General Appearance The Irish Setter is an active, aristocratic bird-dog, rich red in colour, substantial yet elegant in build. Standing over two feet tall at the shoulder, the dog has a straight, fine, glossy coat, longer on ears, chest, tail, and back of legs. Afield he is a swift-moving hunter; at home, a sweet-natured, trainable companion. His is a rollicking personality.

Head Long and lean, its length at least double the width between the ears. The brow is raised, showing a distinct stop midway between the tip of nose and the well-defined occiput (rear point of skull). Thus the nearly level line from occiput to brow is set a little above, and parallel to, the straight and equal line from eye to nose. The skull is oval when viewed from above or front; very slightly domed when viewed in profile. Beauty of head is emphasised by delicate chiseling along the muzzle, around and below the eyes, and along the cheeks. Muzzle moderately deep, nostrils wide, jaws of nearly equal length. Upper lips fairly square but not pendulous, the underline of the jaws being almost parallel with the top line of the muzzle. The teeth meet in a scissors bite in which the upper incisors fit closely over the lower, or they may meet evenly.

Nose Black or chocolate.

Eyes Somewhat almond-shaped, of medium size, placed rather well apart; neither deep-set nor bulging. Color, dark to medium brown. Expression soft yet alert.

Ears Set well back and low, not above level of eye. Leather thin, hanging in a neat fold close to the head, and nearly long enough to reach the nose.

Neck Moderately long, strong but not thick, and slightly arched; free from throatiness, and fitting smoothly into the shoulders.

Body Sufficiently long to permit a straight and free stride. Shoulder blades long, wide, sloping well back, fairly close together at the top, and joined in front to long upper arms angled to bring the elbows slightly rearward along the brisket. Chest deep, reaching approximately to the elbows; rather narrow in front. Ribs

well sprung. Loins of moderate length, muscular and slightly arched. Top line of body from withers to tail slopes slightly downward without sharp drop at the croup. Hindquarters should be wide and powerful with broad, well-developed thighs.

Legs and feet   All legs sturdy, with plenty of bone, and strong, nearly straight pastern. Feet rather small, very firm, toes arched and close. Forelegs straight and sinewy, the elbows moving freely. Hind legs long and muscular from hip to hock, short and nearly perpendicular from hock to ground; well angulated at stifle and hock joints, which, like the elbows, incline neither in nor out.

Tail   Strong at root, tapering to a fine point, about long enough to reach the hock. Carriage straight or curving slightly upward, nearly level with the back.

Coat   Short and fine on head, forelegs, and tips of ears; on all other parts, of moderate length and flat. Feathering long and silky on ears; on back of forelegs and thighs long and fine, with a pleasing fringe of hair on belly and brisket extending onto the chest. Feet well feathered between the toes. Fringe on tail moderately long and tapering. All coat and feathering as straight and free as possible from curl and wave.

Color   Mahogany or rich chestnut red, with no trace of black. A small amount of white on chest, throat, or toes, or a narrow centred streak on skull, is not to be penalized.

Size   There is no disqualification as to size. The make and fit of all parts and their overall balance in the animal are rated more important. Twentyseven inches at the withers with a show weight of about 70 pounds is considered ideal for a dog; the bitch 25 inches, 60 pounds. Variance beyond an inch up or down to be discouraged.

Gait   At the trot the gait is big, very lively, graceful and efficient. The head is held high. The hindquarters drive smoothly and with great power. The forelegs reach well ahead as if to pull in the ground, without giving the appearance of a hackney gait. The dog runs as he stands: straight. Seen from the front or rear, the forelegs, as well as the hind legs below the hock joint, move perpendicularly to the ground, with some tendency towards a

Opposite: Dentition, showing the scissors bite.

single track as speed increases. But a crossing or weaving of the legs, front or back, is objectionable.

Balance   At his best the lines of the Irish Setter so satisfy in overall balance that artists have termed him the most beautiful of all dogs. The correct specimen always exhibits balance whether standing or in motion. Each part of the dog flows and fits smoothly into its neighbouring parts without calling attention to itself.

8

BREEDING

IF YOU have a bitch, you may be very tempted to breed from her, and it is indeed a very natural temptation. Before you go ahead, however, you should give the matter very serious thought. If you have been showing her with some degree of success and have some contacts in the dog world, then there may be some justification for going ahead with a litter, but do still consider the problems that may arise. If yours is purely a pet bitch and your thought is to breed a litter simply for your own amusement or in the mistaken belief that a litter is necessary for the bitch's physical or mental well-being, then the idea is to be discouraged. Again, some people breed a litter thinking that they are going to make a lot of money out of it. This is a mistake, as there are no fortunes to be made from breeding dogs; indeed, a litter can prove costly and heartbreaking. Here are some very important points to consider:

1. You will need space for the puppies, with access to a secure outside run for them.
2. The puppies will need plenty of warmth and if they are born in the winter they will need constant heat, even while the bitch is with them.
3. Vet's bills will be expensive. The bitch may need specialist care and, even if all is well, a visit from the vet will be necessary to check on the well-being of bitch and puppies soon after whelping, and also a later visit to remove dew claws.
4. For at least five weeks the puppies will need a great deal of food between them. This must be the best food, so it will be expensive. Don't forget young puppies have voracious appetites!
5. The market for Irish Setters is not always good. Many people feel that they just cannot afford to keep a dog of this size, so despite costly advertising you may find yourself with half a dozen puppies that you cannot sell and cannot afford to keep. You may be forced

to give them away to maybe unsuitable homes, or even, tragically, to have them put down.

6. Your responsibilities might not end with the sale of the puppies—be prepared for at least one of them to be returned to you on some pretext, such as 'we couldn't give the dog enough exercise', 'he's too expensive to keep', 'he is destructive', 'we are going abroad to live', 'we are moving into a flat where we aren't allowed to keep a dog', 'one of us has become allergic to the dog'. There are many possible reasons or excuses, despite the fact that you may initially have warned the prospective purchaser of the possible pitfalls. So you may be faced with the problem of having to take one or two of the puppies back at some stage.

7. Expect to spend upwards of £150 on the breeding of an average-sized litter. Hopefully you will cover your costs, but how much you make on top of this depends entirely on individual circumstances, for example, how quickly you sell the puppies, how much you have to spend on veterinary bills and advertising, etc.

If you are sure that you have the necessary facilities and can afford all the expenses that may arise, then by all means consider breeding from your bitch.

Do not allow a bitch to have her first litter if she is over five years of age, or under eighteen months of age, and never mate a bitch on her first season. The ideal time for her to have a first litter is between two and three years of age.

Before you do anything else you must check on the health of your bitch. Ask your vet to give her a thorough 'medical' so that you are sure she is physically healthy enough to undergo the strain of pregnancy and whelping. If your bitch has any serious condition which the vet considers hereditary, then you must *on no account* breed from her. It is advisable to check with her breeder that none of her recent ancestors suffered from any serious hereditary condition.

Choice of mate

It is very important that you give careful thought and considera-tion to the choice of a mate for your bitch. You will probably be able to get some advice from the person who bred her. If you have no-one to advise you, then it will pay you to contact a well-known breeder, who may have a really good dog at stud. Guard against using the pet Irish Setter that lives down the road. He may be a very nice dog with a good pedigree, but even so he may be quite unsuitable as a mate for your bitch. If you really do want to use him, then at least contact someone with a good knowledge of Irish Setter pedigrees to advise you on the matter, and be sure that the dog, like your bitch, suffers from no hereditary complaint. Also you must check that your bitch, and the dog of your choice, are on the Kennel Club Active Register.

As regards pedigree, the best choice of dog will probably be one which shares some common ancestry with your bitch, but is not too closely related. Of course, you must also like the look of the dog and it is best if you can find a dog who possesses some good qualities that your bitch may lack. If you use a dog which is not closely related to your bitch, the puppies are likely to be generally of mixed type, but sound (this kind of breeding is called an 'outcross'). If, as advised, you use a dog which is related, but not too closely so, the puppies will still be sound but may be more of a certain type (this is known as 'line breeding'). Finally, if you use a dog which is very closely related to your bitch—as close as half-brother or even closer—the resulting puppies will be far more uniform in type, and good and bad points may be much more accentuated. It is therefore best to leave this kind of breeding ('in-breeding') to the experts, who have sufficient knowledge and experience to carry this out successfully.

The mating

Having decided upon the dog, you must be sure that his owner is agreeable for him to be used on your bitch, so make sure about this well before your bitch comes in season. The dog's owner may well wish to see your bitch and study her pedigree before making a decision. Once the owner of the dog has consented to the proposed mating and has informed you as to the stud fee, etc., it is then up to you to let him know as soon as your bitch comes in season, so that the dog's services can be reserved for her at the appropriate time. This is usually the 10th to 12th day from the onset of the red discharge. However, bitches can vary, and some may be ready earlier or later. A bitch is generally 'ready' when she shows willingness to be mated, by lifting her tail to one side, especially when stroked near the root of her tail.

The ideal situation is one in which the dog and bitch are allowed to run together for several days, as the bitch will usually be much more willing to accept the dog in these circumstances. Some stud dog owners are willing to board the bitch for the days concerned; as long as the bitch is happy about this, it is an ideal arrangement.

A 'maiden' bitch, that is, one that has not been mated before, may show some reluctance to be mated, and someone may have to hold her head while the mating takes place. Some bitches may object strongly, and if the dog is not experienced this could prove traumatic for both, in which case it may be advisable to abandon the idea of mating them—at least for that day. It may be that the bitch is not yet quite ready for mating, or maybe a different dog will have to be tried—if a suitable choice is available. However, if the bitch is obviously nervous or unhappy, it is unfair to force the mating against her will. But, in the majority of cases, a mating does take place. Usually when the dog has mated the bitch there is a 'tie'—the animals remain locked together for anything from 10 to 50 minutes. Conception is most likely to occur when there is a tie, but will often occur without one.

Pre-natal care

Pregnancy is generally 63 to 64 days in duration (see *Gestation Table*). You will not be able to tell whether your bitch is in whelp for a while. An examination by the vet at around the 22nd or 23rd day after mating may reveal some enlargement of the womb, but after this time even a vet will not be able to tell if she is pregnant as the whelps go up under her ribs at about the 24th day and there will be no other obvious signs until the bitch is five to six weeks in whelp, except, maybe, increased pinkness of the teats.

Irrespective of whether you think she is in whelp or not, you must start to increase the bitch's food from about the fifth week onwards. She should receive double her normal amount of food, plus a cereal and milk meal in the morning. She will also need a calcium supplement such as 'Stress'.

Continue to exercise her as usual, but try to prevent her from

GESTATION TABLE

Mated January	Puppies due March	Mated February	Puppies due April	Mated March	Puppies due May	Mated April	Puppies due June	Mated May	Puppies due July	Mated June	Puppies due August	Mated July	Puppies due September	Mated August	Puppies due October	Mated September	Puppies due November	Mated October	Puppies due December	Mated November	Puppies due January	Mated December	Puppies due February
1	5	1	5	1	3	1	3	1	3	1	3	1	2	1	3	1	3	1	3	1	3	1	2
2	6	2	6	2	4	2	4	2	4	2	4	2	3	2	4	2	4	2	4	2	4	2	3
3	7	3	7	3	5	3	5	3	5	3	5	3	4	3	5	3	5	3	5	3	5	3	4
4	8	4	8	4	6	4	6	4	6	4	6	4	5	4	6	4	6	4	6	4	6	4	5
5	9	5	9	5	7	5	7	5	7	5	7	5	6	5	7	5	7	5	7	5	7	5	6
6	10	6	10	6	8	6	8	6	8	6	8	6	7	6	8	6	8	6	8	6	8	6	7
7	11	7	11	7	9	7	9	7	9	7	9	7	8	7	9	7	9	7	9	7	9	7	8
8	12	8	12	8	10	8	10	8	10	8	10	8	9	8	10	8	10	8	10	8	10	8	9
9	13	9	13	9	11	9	11	9	11	9	11	9	10	9	11	9	11	9	11	9	11	9	10
10	14	10	14	10	12	10	12	10	12	10	12	10	11	10	12	10	12	10	12	10	12	10	11
11	15	11	15	11	13	11	13	11	13	11	13	11	12	11	13	11	13	11	13	11	13	11	12
12	16	12	16	12	14	12	14	12	14	12	14	12	13	12	14	12	14	12	14	12	14	12	13
13	17	13	17	13	15	13	15	13	15	13	15	13	14	13	15	13	15	13	15	13	15	13	14
14	18	14	18	14	16	14	16	14	16	14	16	14	15	14	16	14	16	14	16	14	16	14	15
15	19	15	19	15	17	15	17	15	17	15	17	15	16	15	17	15	17	15	17	15	17	15	16
16	20	16	20	16	18	16	18	16	18	16	18	16	17	16	18	16	18	16	18	16	18	16	17
17	21	17	21	17	19	17	19	17	19	17	19	17	18	17	19	17	19	17	19	17	19	17	18
18	22	18	22	18	20	18	20	18	20	18	20	18	19	18	20	18	20	18	20	18	20	18	19
19	23	19	23	19	21	19	21	19	21	19	21	19	20	19	21	19	21	19	21	19	21	19	20
20	24	20	24	20	22	20	22	20	22	20	22	20	21	20	22	20	22	20	22	20	22	20	21
21	25	21	25	21	23	21	23	21	23	21	23	21	22	21	23	21	23	21	23	21	23	21	22
22	26	22	26	22	24	22	24	22	24	22	24	22	23	22	24	22	24	22	24	22	24	22	23
23	27	23	27	23	25	23	25	23	25	23	25	23	24	23	25	23	25	23	25	23	25	23	24
24	28	24	28	24	26	24	26	24	26	24	26	24	25	24	26	24	26	24	26	24	26	24	25
25	29	25	29	25	27	25	27	25	27	25	27	25	26	25	27	25	27	25	27	25	27	25	26
26	30	26	30	26	28	26	28	26	28	26	28	26	27	26	28	26	28	26	28	26	28	26	27
27	31	27	MAY 1	27	29	27	29	27	29	27	29	27	28	27	29	27	29	27	29	27	29	27	28
28	APRIL 1	28	2	28	30	28	30	28	30	28	30	28	29	28	30	28	30	28	30	28	30	28	MAR 1
29	2	29	3	29	31	29	JULY 1	29	31	29	31	29	30	29	31	29	DEC 1	29	31	29	31	29	2
30	3	—	—	30	JUNE 1	30	2	30	AUG 1	30	SEP 1	30	OCT 1	30	NOV 1	30	2	30	JAN 1	30	FEB 1	30	3
31	4	—	—	31	2	—	—	31	2	—	—	31	2	31	2	—	—	31	2	—	—	31	4

Showing when your bitch is due to whelp

over-exertion, especially from jumping over any high obstacle. The bitch should be wormed around the second or third week of pregnancy, certainly no later.

When she is five to six weeks in whelp, some swelling of the abdomen may be noticeable, but it is not always so. From seven weeks onwards the pregnancy should be more obvious and you may be able to detect the movement of the puppies. At this stage it is a good idea to ring your vet and inform him of the imminent 'confinement', so that he will be prepared in advance for a call from you.

If the bitch shows no signs of pregnancy by the seventh week ask the vet to take a look at her. She may have a very small litter, or she may have no pups at all. Bitches also sometimes reabsorb their puppies. It is disappointing when a bitch 'misses' but this does not mean that she will not produce pups if mated again at another season. Most stud dog owners will offer a free stud if the bitch misses, although this is not obligatory.

You will need to make or acquire a whelping box well in advance. This should be made of wood and approximately 4 ft square, with sides 9 to 12 inches high. A guard rail inside the box, allowing young puppies to crawl away from the mother if she is squashing them, is a good idea.

The bitch should be introduced to her whelping box several weeks before she is due to whelp. She should be encouraged to sniff around it, sit in it, or even sleep in it if she so wishes. Keep it in the room where you wish the whelping to take place.

Anything that you consider could be abnormal should be reported to the vet without delay, especially any excessive or offensive vaginal discharge during pregnancy.

For the actual whelping you will need lots and lots of newspaper (start collecting this weeks before she is due to have the puppies). This will also be needed in abundance to line the puppies' living quarters. You should also have at the ready several old, but clean, towels, disinfectant (Dettol), some sterilised scissors, a large cardboard box and a hot-water bottle, a drinking bowl, some milk, and maybe a drop of brandy.

Whelping
I do not propose in this book to discuss in detail the intricacies of

whelping—the subject is long and complicated and I strongly advise you to read a specialised book on the subject. I would also advise you to contact someone who has plenty of experience with whelping bitches and who may be willing to assist you with the actual whelping. A vet's attendance during the birth could be extremely costly and is not necessary provided that everything is straightforward, which it generally is with Irish Setters. However, a visit from the vet is vital if there are any complications and will be necessary anyway for the routine post-natal check within 24 hours of whelping.

Here are a few brief details of what to expect when your bitch has her puppies.

From around her 61st or 62nd day she will probably be extremely restless and you may feel you need to stay up all night with her while she scratches round her whelping box and vigorously tears up the newspaper! You will probably think that she is about to start labour any minute, but you could be in for quite a long wait.

A useful sign of imminent whelping is a drop in temperature by a couple of degrees during the 24 hours prior to commencement of labour. She will probably refuse food at this time also. She may behave in a very restless manner for a couple of days before anything happens. Many bitches don't whelp until the 64th day, but if this day passes without event it is advisable to contact the vet in case there is some obstruction.

When the contractions actually start she will pant a lot and her breathing may be irregular. You may be able to see the rise and fall of her abdomen with the contractions.

When the first puppy is imminent the bitch will start to strain— this will be quite unmistakeable. Should she continue to strain in this way for an hour without the arrival of a puppy, contact the vet immediately—this applies whether it is the first puppy or the last. Any delay in treatment in this situation could prove very serious.

The bitch may experience some pain when passing the first puppy, but it should not take too long. The water bag containing the puppy will be seen slowly emerging; it may burst before she has pushed it out, or it may come out intact. Some bitches know instinctively how to tear this open, but others, particularly first-time whelpers, may make no attempt to do so. If this is the case you must act promptly and tear the bag open yourself, or the puppy may drown in the fluid.

If the puppy does not cry immediately, it may need some help with breathing. Pick the puppy up, gently clean the mucous from its mouth and make sure the airways are clear; then shake it fairly vigorously, with a downwards motion, to get the fluid out of its lungs. Support the head and neck while doing this, to avoid injury. The bitch will immediately start to lick the puppy in quite a rough manner, instinctively trying to get it to breathe. If the puppy still does not react, as a final means of resuscitation, you can try breathing, very gently, into its mouth through a small tube of some kind. You must do this with great care, as the lungs of a tiny puppy could easily be ruptured by too much pressure of air.

The umbilical cord will still be attached to the afterbirth, which the bitch may not have passed yet. She may try to bite through the cord, and at the same time pull out and eat the afterbirth, but make sure that, when she does this, the puppy is not left suspended by its own cord for too long, or the result could be an umbilical hernia. If you are worried about the time taken by all this, you can tear the umbilical cord yourself (about one inch from where it joins the body), or cut it with the sterilised scissors, but tearing it is preferable, as there will be less bleeding.

Check the number of afterbirths passed with the number of puppies. You will want to know how many afterbirths have been passed so that you will know if any has been retained, as if this happens a severe infection can result.

Put the newly arrived puppy to one of the teats as soon as possible. The bitch will be happy to let it suckle. The time lapse between the arrival of each puppy is quite variable—it can be as short as a minute or as long as half an hour or more. You will know when the next one is imminent, as the bitch will again become restless and start straining. The puppy that is already born will have to be taken from her temporarily, for its own safety, and should be placed in a cardboard box in which there is a warm hot-water bottle wrapped in towels, so that it can be kept warm. This procedure will be repeated with the existing pups each time another one arrives.

. . . and with another young friend

Setters in natural surroundings

A formal showing

An informal showing

The number of puppies can vary enormously—from one to, the record number for an Irish Setter, twentytwo! If the whelping is still continuing after 12 hours, it is advisable to call the vet; he should be able to tell how many, if any, pups are still inside her. She will probably be very exhausted by this time and may need a drink of milk with a drop of brandy. She may also need to spend a penny (this need can arise at any time during her whelping), so try to persuade her to go outside to relieve herself.

Post-natal care

When she has finished whelping and seems content to suckle her pups, providing that the milk has arrived in the teats and there is nothing else amiss, leave her for an hour or two before calling out the vet. If she has whelped late at night, leave it till the morning, provided all seems well. In rare circumstances, the milk may not come down and urgent veterinary treatment will be required to make it do so, for the pups will soon die without nourishment.

A routine part of the veterinary visit will also be an injection of pituitrin, to help her expel any retained afterbirth, or even an unborn puppy, if the vet thinks one is still inside her.

If she has had more than ten pups you will have to make the difficult decision of whether to keep them all or not. No bitch can be expected to rear more than ten, so the rest will have to be hand reared, or a foster mother will have to be found for them. Hand rearing can be an exhausting business, and it may be best to have some of the new born pups put down shortly after birth. However, some vets consider this unethical, so you may be left with no choice but to rear them by hand. If you find yourself in this position, you would be well advised to obtain a specialised book on puppy rearing and follow the instructions given therein. Your vet will also advise you.

The bitch should be given some warm milk with glucose when she has finished whelping, and for the first 48 hours she should receive plenty of calcium-containing meals, such as scrambled eggs and milk pudding. Don't give her any meat for a day or so. After this time her diet must be a very nourishing one to give her all the reserves she needs to feed all those pups! She will need four meals a day: two of milk and cereal or rice pudding, and two meat meals, with approximately 1½lb of meat and biscuit in each. Make sure she has plenty of clean water to drink.

If the bitch appears unwell in any way during the days and weeks following whelping, seek veterinary advice. Watch out for signs of Eclampsia, a condition caused by calcium deficiency which causes fits and can quickly prove fatal. If you notice that the bitch is shaking or rigid, has a glazed expression or is in a state of collapse, she could well be suffering from Eclampsia, and immediate treatment will be necessary.

Puppy care and registration

If the puppies are whelped in your living room or kitchen, it will be advisable to move them to somewhere more suitable within 24 hours or so. Some place where an infra-red lamp can be suspended a couple of feet above the whelping box will be ideal. The puppies will need constant warmth, especially at night, when a puppy which crawls away from the warmth of its mother could die of cold. The lamp will be needed all day for the first few weeks, except in hot weather, and all night, summer and winter, for the first six to eight weeks. Do take care, however, if the puppies are born in the summer, to see that their accommodation does not become over-heated—this can easily happen if the youngsters are kept in a conservatory, or something similar. Puppies can easily die from heat stroke. So be constantly on your guard against extremes of temperature.

The puppies are blind for the first ten days or so of life, and the eyes will open gradually from about this time. You must be prepared for the occasional fatality in the litter during the first few weeks. The bitch may unwittingly roll on a puppy and kill it, while some puppies with congenital abnormalities may be rejected by the mother. If you notice milk coming down a puppy's nose, it is as well to check whether the puppy has a cleft palate. Another possibility is a condition of the oesophagus, whereby milk is brought back due to lack of muscle tone. If the latter is the case, little can be done to remedy it, unfortunately. Be guided by your vet, as one condition can easily be confused with another at this young age.

Dew claws must be removed during the first four or five days.

Get the vet or someone experienced to do this. It seems very cruel, but is nevertheless necessary, for dew claws can cause great problems in later life if not removed. Remove the bitch from the pups while the dew claws are being removed and try to keep her well out of earshot. The puppies will cry more out of fear than pain and will be perfectly all right within a couple of minutes.

The bitch will have a dark discharge for some days after giving birth, but if this begins to smell offensive or is very heavy, contact the vet.

You will need a good stock of newspaper to line the whelping box and this, as you will find, will need changing frequently. Soiled paper will have to be burned regularly for the sake of hygiene. The puppies' nails are soft, and should be trimmed regularly at the tips to prevent them from scratching the bitch as, if left untrimmed, they can act like little razors.

Puppies need worming several times before they leave the litter. These days, initial worming can be started as early as three weeks with 'Erliworm', with a further dose at six weeks. When the worms have been passed, they should be burned without delay.

From about three weeks of age, the puppies can start to be weaned. Get them to lap milk from a saucer (they will want to paddle in it at first!). Do not give them cow's milk at this early age as it is not sufficiently concentrated. Special dried milk powder (Lactol for example) can be obtained from pet shops and other suppliers of dog food. Make sure that you make the powder up exactly to the instructions on the tin or packet. Introduce raw scraped beef or soft tinned dog food and to this can be gradually added soaked puppy meal. While they are still being fed by their mother they can receive two meat meals a day, plus milk. By four to five weeks they should be weaned from her altogether and receiving four meals a day—two meat and biscuit and two cereal and milk, or milk pudding. 'Stress' or similar should be added, for building strong teeth and bones. By the time the pups are eight weeks old they should each be receiving daily: 1 pint milk with cereal (cow's milk will be acceptable by now if wished), ½lb meat and ¼lb puppy meal, divided between the four meals. Clean water should always be available.

When the puppies are weaned, the bitch's milk will need to be dried up. Cut down on her fluids and also on her food. If, after a couple of days, she is still uncomfortable and continuing to make a lot of milk, tablets may be needed from the vet. As these tablets contain hormones, do not allow her near the puppies until the milk has completely dried up.

Now to the paper work. If you wish to register the puppies under your own prefix, you must apply for this to the Kennel Club long before you breed the litter as your application may take several months to be processed. Even if you do not wish to bother with your own prefix, you should contact the Kennel Club before your bitch is mated in order to obtain the relevant forms for recording the litter and registering the puppies on the 'Basic' or 'Active' register. As Kennel Club procedures are apt to change from time to time, it is best to ask their advice regarding these matters, but a full explanation of how to register the puppies is given on the forms.

Selling your puppies

Start advertising the puppies when they are about six weeks old. You can advertise them in your local paper and in the specialist dog papers. Do be careful who you sell your puppies to. Make sure that you explain to the prospective buyers all the drawbacks of owning an Irish Setter and fight shy of anyone who lives in a flat, goes out to work all day, or buys a bitch thinking they are going to make a lot of money by breeding from her.

You may be able to obtain pedigree forms from your local pet shop. If not, you can obtain them at large dog shows or from advertisements in the dog papers. Make sure that you fill out the pedigree forms accurately as a mistake could cause untold confusion.

You must ask the purchasers to leave a deposit. Give them a receipt for this and another receipt later for the balance, when they take the puppy away. You should also provide a certificate of worming (available from PRO Dogs). You will have to make out diet sheets for the puppies and give one of these to each of the new owners.

The puppies will be ready to go to their new homes at eight

Opposite: Could you part company with any of this happy trio?

weeks of age and hopefully they will all have been sold by this time. The asking price is up to you and it is a good idea to check with other Irish Setter breeders as to what they are asking for their puppies. Of course, your prices should vary a little from puppy to puppy. In other words, you will probably want to ask more for the potentially show-worthy puppies than for those which do not look so promising, although this is something which it is not always easy to assess at this age. It is a very good idea to ask an experienced breeder to come and pick out what he or she considers to be the best dog and best bitch when the puppies are seven to eight weeks old.

Incidentally, should any of the puppies be going abroad, you should contact the Ministry of Agriculture in London for details of the particular country's requirements regarding innoculations and health certificates, all of which will have to be given or obtained before the puppy leaves the country. This means, in effect, that you will have to keep the puppy until it is old enough to receive the various vaccinations, etc. You will also have to obtain an Export Pedigree from the Kennel Club.

Parting company
Puppies are extremely hard work, but they are most rewarding. If you are going to keep one of them yourself, then parting with the others may not be quite so upsetting, but be prepared nevertheless for some heart-rending. Do ask the new owners to keep you informed of progress and to come back to you for any help or advice which they might require. They will really appreciate this.

Always make sure that you have the address of everyone who has a puppy from you. You never know when you may wish to get in touch with them about something or other, or you may wish to contact them to put your own mind at rest that all is well with the puppy. If you are a conscientious breeder and love your puppies, then concern about the well-being of any of them can cause many a sleepless night! Of course, you must not keep pestering the new owners, but I am sure that they will always be grateful for your interest and concern.

9

A BRIEF HISTORY OF THE BREED

SPACE DOES not allow us to deal at any length with the evolution of the Irish Setter, a subject which other books deal splendidly with and in great detail. Most first-time owners, however, do appreciate a brief summary of the origins of the breed.

Evidence suggests that the Irish Setter evolved by specific breeding and selection from an amalgam of various other breeds, or crosses of breeds and the most probable ancestors and/or relatives would seem to be the other Setters, such as the English and Gordon, the Pointer, Bloodhound, Irish Water Spaniel, and maybe some other varieties of spaniel.

The breed was definitely established by around 1800, although the Irish Setter of those days was rather different from the one we know today. At that time it was red and white in colour, while some even had black markings. Later, colour became a source of much controversy between individual breeders. Some preferred a predominance of white, others favoured the solid red colour as we know it today. Even now, the red and white Irish Setter still exists in Ireland, but as an entirely separate breed. The early breeders of Irish Setters were mainly aristocrats and sportsmen. The dog show was unknown at that time and the dogs were bred purely for sport. So the working qualities of certain strains were as important then as the show qualities are these days. The first ever dog show in this country was held in Newcastle upon Tyne in 1859, and was for Setters and Pointers only. So from this time onwards the Irish Setter was valued for its qualities as a show dog as well as its working ability.

Probably the most famous Irish Setter of the last century was Ch. Palmerston, born about 1862. He was very refined and elegant, with a strip of white on his forehead, which became rather fashionable. He was certainly a legend in his own lifetime, and was used so extensively at stud that today there can hardly be

71

an Irish Setter alive which does not trace back to him on many lines.

The Irish Setter continued to enjoy great popularity during the early part of the twentieth century, until a hereditary condition, Progressive Retinal Atrophy, known by some as 'night blindness', became apparent. It appeared gradually, over a number of years, until the situation was deemed so serious that positive steps had to be taken to eliminate it. PRA was such a serious scourge that it threatened the very existence of the breed. Fortunately the dedication and integrity of the breeders of that time almost completely eliminated the condition due to intensive test-matings to ascertain whether dogs and bitches were 'carriers' of the condition.

Today the Irish Setter enjoys an unparalleled popularity and those of us who now know the joy of owning one have to thank the breeders of the past who saved it from possible obscurity.

Opposite: Today the Irish Setter enjoys an unparalleled popularity.

10

GENERAL INFORMATION

THE ADDRESS of the Kennel Club is: 1 Clarges Street, London W1Y
8AB. The Kennel Club can provide addresses of the following
breed clubs, all of which can be of great interest to the Irish Setter
owner, whatever his special interest in the breed may be:

Irish Setter Association of England
Irish Setter Breeders Club
Irish Setter Club of Scotland
Irish Setter Club of Wales
South of England Irish Setter Club
Belfast and District Irish Setter Club
Ulster Irish Red Setter Club
The Setter and Pointer Club
Northern Counties Pointer and Setter Society
Pointer and Setter Society

The addresses of these various associations have not been given
here as details are bound to change from time to time.

Other societies and associations which may be of some use
include:

PRO Dogs
National Canine Defence League
National Dog Owners' Association
Dog Breeders Associates

The Kennel Club can also provide you with the addresses of
these organisations.

For those not residing in the United Kingdom, the following
addresses may be of some interest:

The American Kennel Club, 51 Madison Avenue, New York, N.Y. 10010

Canadian Kennel Club, 111 Eglington Avenue East, Toronto 12, Ontario

Australian National Kennel Council, Royal Show Grounds, Ascot Vale, Victoria

INDEX